SRI KRISHNAMRUTA MAHARNAVA-THROUGHWAY TO HAPPINESS

DR.SURESH KUMAR RUDRAHITHLU

Sri Sri Sri. Mahavatar Babaji & ISKCON Founder Sri. A.C.Bhaktivedanta Swamy Prabhupada

My ancestor Sri.Yadapadithaya at whose residence Madhwacharya had written this book.

My beloved Parents Late R.S.Yadapadithaya Shishila

&

Late.Premalatha

Contents

Acknowledgements

1. Sankeerna Granthagalu – Akhila Bharata Madhwa Mahamandala – 2007

2. Sadacharasmruti – Sri Krishnamruta Maharnava – Ananda Balaga – 2013

3. Krishnanemba Sodeya Kadalu – Dr Bannanje Govindacharya – Ishavasya Prathishtana – 2015

4. Sumadhwa Vijaya – by Sri Narayana Panditacharya

5.Srimadanandatirtha Bhagavatpada's Sri Krishnamruta Maharnava- by Sri.Hariprasad Nellitheertha-2018

Krishnamruta Maharnava is one of the 37 (main) works composed by Sri Madhwacharya. It is part of what is known as the "Sarvamoola Granthas". This work contains more than 220 shlokas and is mainly a collation of vaishnava shlokas from various puranas. The shlokas reaffirm various practices mandated for a vaishnava. They also elucidate the importance of being a vaishnava, the chief duties and the benefits of vaishnavatva. The work contains important instructions on following ekadashi, the importance of worshipping shaligrama and chakranika, the greatness of gopichandana and various other topics. It is an important source of information for any mAdhwa and in fact any vaishnava.

The **Sumadhwavijaya** gives some details about the circumstances behind the composition of the Krishnamruta Maharnava. Towards the end of his stay on earth, Sri Madhwa once visited a dhanvantari kshetra known as kokkada in Dakshina Kannada. Here, he was welcomed and worshipped by a brahmana known as **Yadapadithaya** the ancestor of author of this book. Since he belonged to the bhagavatha sampradaya which followed the panchayatana mode of worship **Yadapadithaya** had numerous questions about the accuracy of the **madhwa** mode of worship and interpretation of scriptures. Hence he requested **Sri Madhwacharya** to provide him, and his family, guidance on the same. In order to assuage the concerns of his devotee, and also to ensure no vaishnava sustains any doubt in future, **Sri Madhwacharya** composed the **SriKrishnamrutha Maharnava** which was, by design, a collection of **purana shlokas**.

Since the puranas are a valid pramana, there could never be any doubt about the validity of what is given in the same. Thus, **Sri Madhwacharya** blessed the followers of the **dvaita sampradaya** and **vaishnavas** in general with yet another masterpiece work to aid them on their path to sadhana and eventually moksha

1.He – who is worshipped, remembered, meditated upon, praised, is the topic of discourses, who is the giver of salvation – I bow to that Keshava, the controller of even Brahma and Rudra.

2.In order to help the world, which is suffering from the three fold misery of Adhyatmika, Adibhoutika and Adidaivika troubles, and to help achieve peace and happiness, I am narrating the ocean of nectar of Sri Krishna (Srikrishnamruta Maharnava).

Hari deeksha & Greatness of Hari Puja

3. One who doesn't take Deeksha (initiation) into Sri Hari ('s worship) and who doesn't pray & worship Him – he is like an animal in this world. What is the purpose of such a life? Note: Starting from this shloka, several shlokas cited from various puranas lay special emphasis on the 'archana' of Lord Hari .

4.In this life, which is full of big miseries such as birth, disease, fear etc, the worship of Adhokshaja is the only big fortune.

5. Vishnu is inside all and is the controller of all. He is also the refuge for all. One who pleases Him through his worship – he alone is the fortunate one in this world. Such a person alone will bring glory to his lineage.

6. More than Yagnas, Tapas and other daily (routine and good) activities, it is the continuous worship of Lord Hari that will lead humans towards salvation (Moksha).

7.The worship of Lord Hari leads to the destruction of ignorance caused by Kali and the removal of all sins. A person who does such daily worship of the Lord is also to be revered – just like Vishnu himself .

8. O Muni! In this Kali Yuga, when Tamasa Guna is all pervading, there is nothing more beneficial for Jivas than the worship of Lord Hari. Therefore, those who are eligible for salvation always worship Him .

9.Lord Hari is all pervading. He is always ornate with Shankha, Chakra and Gada. He is the controller of even Brahma (and others) who are the controllers of Indra and other devatas. Hence, if Vishnu is worshipped, in effect, all the others are also worshipped!

10.Keshava is the Lord of the Universe, one who is worshipped by devatas such as Brahma and Shiva and asuras such as Prahlada, one who destroyed Kamsa & Keshi, one who is the controller of Brahma and Rudra; One who worships Him with complete devotion will never be condemned to hell.

11. Shankara said:: Even if one worships Govinda only once (for those in great difficulty) with Bilvapatra (read Tulasi), such a person will become eligible for Moksha. Such a person will be free from troubles and will later reside in Vaikunta and other Vishnu Lokas eternally.

12. Shankara said:: One who worships Janardana, the Lord of all Lords, at least once with complete devotion is indeed blessed and such a person will attain the highest position of Moksha.

13. One who worships or prays to the Lord at least once, even for the sake of fun, will attain Vaikunta, which is otherwise difficult to attain even for Devatas

14. Narada said:: The main purpose/reward of the human life is to worship that Vishnu who is the Lord of the Universe, who is the Lord of even devatas such as Brahma and Rudra, who is the holder of Sharnga (bow) and who has all the auspicious attributes.

15. Pulastya said:: If one worships Purushottama with devotion, albeit offering just blades of Kusha grass, Hari definitely grants such a person fruits (results) much more than what even Yagnas can fetch!

16.If one worships Hari even only with water, He, who is the controller of all the Gods and who wears Shankha and Chakra, grants results very easily.

17. For those suffering in hell, Dharma (Yama) asks – "How come you did not worship Hari, the one who relieves us from miseries and who is the Lord of even Brahma and Rudra.

18. Yama asks:: "How come Vishnu, the one who took the form of Narasimha, one who is the controller of all senses (Hrishikesha), who has eyes which resemble Lotus petals, and who grants salvation to those who merely think of Him, was never worshipped by you?"

Note: Starting from this shloka, the following several shlokas highlight the importance of 'smarana' of Lord Hari.

19. "Why did you not worship Vishnu who grants His place (Moksha) even if one worships him with just plain water (when other materials are unavailable)?"

20. Brahma said:: Initiation as a Vaishnava removes all misery. One who does not take such an initiation will always be subjected to the trouble of experiencing birth and death. Such persons will become thieves and will always be condemned.

21. Markandeya said:: One who worships Vishnu, the Lord of Brahma and other devatas and the One who destroys the cycle of birth and death, even once – such a person will surely achieve all his goals. Such a person will attain the highest position of Mukti.

22. O Lord of Indra and other devatas – In order to achieve even one of the Purusharthas among Dharma, Artha, Kama and Moksha, there is no other way than worshipping the Lord. This statement of mine is the truth Notes: This was the vachana of Markandeya to Rudra, whom he addresses as devesha.

23. Rudra said:: Vishnu is the one who has taken the form of Yagnavaraha and He is infinitely radiant. One who worships the Lord – to him also I offer my respects.

24. Marichi said:: O son of the King! One who doesn't worship Govinda will never attain the supreme position of Vaikunta. Therefore, do worship Achyuta.

25. Atri said:: One who receives the grace of Vishnu, who resides in everybody's heart and is greater than even the best devatas such as Brahma – such a person will surely attain the indestructible Vaikunta. What I have said is indeed true!

26. Angira said:: Vishnu, One whose nature is indestructible and who does not undergo growth, decay etc, One within whom the entire Universe resides – do worship Him if you desire to attain the best position.

27.Pulastya said:: Vishnu is the Supreme Personality. He is the main refuge for all. He is full of infinite auspicious attributes and has no beginning nor any end. Those who worship Him obtain Moksha, which is otherwise impossible to obtain.

28. Pulaha said:: O Noble man! You too worship Vishnu, whose worship, through hundred yagas, by Purandara got him the position of the leader of Gods.

29. Those who worship Vishnu get all their desires, related to anything in the three worlds, satisfied. Similarly, they also obtain Vaikunta, which is even better than the three worlds (better than heaven).

30. Those who worship Vishnu, the one who wears Shankha, Chakra and Gada, will lose all their sins and will enter (the abode of) Vishnu, One who is the best and One who is full of auspicious attributes.

31. One who gets liberated from the bondage of this world will enter the form of Aniruddha first; He will then enter the form of Pradyumna, the Supreme amongst all; Next, the soul will enter the form of Samkarshana, the form which is full of activities; Finally, the soul enters the form of Vasudeva, the form which is greater than even Ramaa, Brahma and others.

32. Vedanta has decided that there is nothing greater than Vasudeva. How then can one return to this material world after having reached Vasudeva?

33. Atri said:: Whether it is a (qualified) man, or a woman born in the right Varna (or having the right lakshanas), One who worships Lord Janardana with devotion will have all their good wishes satisfied.

34. Koushika said:: Those people who are undergoing immense suffering due to lack of worship of Govinda, such people can attain eternal bliss (Moksha) by just worshipping Vasudeva.

35. Brahma said:: Who can ever wish to cross the ocean just by the power of their own hands? Similarly, who can ever hope to attain Moksha without worshipping Vasudeva?

36. Parashara said:: If someone commits sin and then repents for it, Shastras have prescribed an atonement for such a person – the remembrance (chanting) of Lord Hari's name!

37. The amount of sin that is burnt away by the mere name of Lord Hari is so much that even the worst sinners cannot commit (that amount of sin)!

38. Brahma said:: Those people who have never committed any good deed (Punya) since many lives, those who do not have any mind, those who are of Tamasic nature; such people in this Universe do not like Bhakti nor chanting and remembering Govinda's name.

39. Only when one gains control over his senses, has a pure heart and chants the name of Lord Hari, does a Purusha get liberated from the cycle of birth, sorrow, ageing and other such sufferings.

40. But, as Kali Yuga progresses, as the knowledge of Dharma reduces, people will not remember nor chant the name of Hari, though it has the power to burn all the sins committed due to the influence of Kali.

41. In Kali Yuga, the ignorant do not worship nor meditate on Lord Hari – One who is the Lord of all Gods, and the one who washes away all our sorrow.

42. One who always remembers Lord Vishnu with sincerity and with a pure heart, such a soul will escape the cycle of life & death and attain the abode of Vishnu.

43. One who remembers Narayana daily will never be troubled by the miseries of life such as gestation, birth, ageing, disease and other sorrows.

44. One who constantly remembers Lord Garudadhwaja will never see the path of Yama nor will they ever see hell – not even in their dreams!

45. A devotee who keeps (remembers) the form of Achyuta in his heart, who always has His name on his lips, feeds Naivedya of Lord Hari to his stomach and keeps the tirtha and Nirmalya on his head, such a person will attain salvation.

46. Just as a mere spark burns down an entire mound of cotton, so does chanting the name of Lord Govinda burn down an entire mountain of sin. Let there be no doubt about this!

47. Agastya said:: Just like the (wings of) mountains were destroyed by the power of Vajrayudha, similarly the cell (jail) that a soul is wrapped in (i.e. Sthoola and Sookshma Shareeras) is destroyed by remembering the name of Lord Krishna.

48. The more qualified souls (Satthvik) are always interested in Lord Krishna. They constantly remember Krishna and are always devoted to Him. Their heart is always on Krishna. Such souls reach Vishnu even though they lose their bodies, just like the Havis (fire-offerings) which reach Agni when offered with Mantras (even though they get burnt outwardly).

49. It is a big mistake and big loss for a human, if he does not remember Vasudeva even for a Muhurtha or second! Such a mistake is equal to blindness (not reading Shastras), laziness (keeping quiet instead of reading His stories) and dumbness (not chanting His name).

50. The realized souls call Narayana as the biggest and most famous thief on this Earth. He steals away all the sins accumulated by a soul over many births, just by mere remembrance of His name!

51. The chanting/remembrance of the name of Lord Vasudeva, the wielder of the Sudarshana Chakra, burns away all the sins accumulated over crores of births!

52. One who meditates every day on Narayana with full concentration and devotion, what is the use of pilgrimages, penances and yagnas for such a person?

Note: Starting here, several shlokas highlight the importance of 'dhyana' in the worship of Lord Hari

53. One who loses interest (renounces) on material objects, obtains the knowledge of hierarchy (taratamya) and chants the name of Narayana, the master (teacher) of the Gods, such people, due to their meditation will lose all the dirt accumulated in their hearts and will never drink their mother's milk again (i.e will never be born again – will attain Mukti).

54. O soul! Always think of Lord Vasudeva as being in this body. Lord Hari, who is always the subject of meditation, will surely destroy the cycle of samsara (birth & death).

Essence of all Shastras:

55. The main conclusion arrived at when all the scriptures were researched and studied in detail was only this – One should always worship/meditate Lord Narayana to obtain salvation!

56. One whose mere remembrance causes a soul to experience (obtain) all auspicious things, I seek refuge in that Hari, the one who has no beginning (birth).

57. The punya, according to Shastras, obtained by studying Vedas, performing Yagnas, penances, donations, observing rituals, pilgrimages, performing Vaishvadeva, building thataka etc – all can be obtained by merely remembering/chanting the name of Lord Vasudeva

58. A person's desire, however small or big it is, will be instantly satisfied, if he worships Lord Vishnu with devotion.

59. O Maitreya! Just as gold and other metals melt away when exposed to fire, similarly all the sins melt away when one chants the name of Hari with devotion .

60. If one chants/sings the name of Lord Hari with devotion, even those sins – which will fetch the sorrow of unbearable hell and which are caused by Kali – will be destroyed

61. Indra and others act as enemies in one's pursuit to obtain Moksha in this easy way. But, one who depends upon Keshava obtains Moksha without any difficulties

62. In the entire Jambudveepa island, surrounded by four oceans, there is none other than Keshava who has the cure for all our sins!

63. The results one obtains by worshipping Lord Hari for 100 years in Kruta Yuga is obtained in Kali Yuga merely by chanting the name of the Lord.

64. But, as Kali Yuga progresses and Dharma reduces, then none will (be able to) chant the name of Achyuta, one who is indestructible and one who grants moksha.

65. Just as animals run away upon hearing a lion's roar, so will all the sins of humans run away upon chanting (knowingly or unknowingly) the name of Lord Hari.

66. Brahma said:: The mantra called "Narayana" exists; The tongue is in one's own control; Still people end up falling in terrible hell. What a surprise!

67. Those who are subject to lots of sufferings; those who are troubled with many miseries; those who are physically incapable; those who are scared (of thieves and others); those who are suffering from terrible diseases; All these people will instantly lose all their trouble and obtain peace and happiness by the mere remembrance and chanting of the name of Narayana.

68. Kaushika said:: One who chants the name of Krishna even once and worships Him will never enter the jail of a mother's womb nor will he ever enter the sorrow filled world of Yama (hell).

69. The attainment of heaven, which is part of a cycle (of birth & death) is on one side. The Japa of Vasudeva, which is the cause of Moksha (and thereby no return) is on the other side. (Is there any comparison?).

70. By whose remembrance and chanting, one is freed from any subsequent birth in this world, one should understand that Lord and constantly chant the two aksharas "Hari".

71. O Tongue of mine, you don't seem to like me. Why are you not saying the name of Lord Hari. O Auspicious one! Say "Hari" at least now. Isn't He the only boat that will take us across the ocean of life?

72. In this world that has no essence, Lord Hari is the one who has more substance/essence than even Lakshmi & Brahma. Just as Chatak birds will not drink water even though it is tasty, similarly the sinned ones will never attain Lord Hari, who is full of essence.

73. For one who has the two syllables constituting "Hari" at the forefront of his tongue, what is the use of Kurukshetra, Kashi, Pushkara and other pilgrim centres?

74. Brahma said:: In this world which is devoid of happiness, there is only one thing that has been proven as the best – the worship of Lord Hari, which (who) gives the best results.

75. Only that tongue that chants the name of Lord Hari is the (real) tongue. Only that mind which resides in him is the real mind. Only that hand which worships him is worthy of praise.

76. One who worships Lord Vishnu with firm devotion, after having controlled his senses, such a person will attain the best position of Vaikunta even if he always stayed at his home only!

77. Shankara said:: O noble one! One who is well versed in Dharma! One who has killed the Danavas! You are asking about the worship of Vishnu. This is really appropriate!.

78. O Bhargava! Those who do not rid themselves of their sins do not feel devotion towards Lord Keshava for a muhurtha or a minute or even half a minute.

79. Only that Manas which resides in Lord Keshava is qualified to obtain Moksha. That being the case, what is the use of a Manas which does not have firm attachment towards Lord Hari, the Lord of Brahma and Rudra?.

Purpose of Indriyas:

80.That tongue which does not chant the name of Lord Hari is not a tongue. It is a tumour in the mouth. Those ears which do not listen to the tales of the Lord are not ears. They are mere perforations!.

81. That tongue which does not praise the glory of Lord Hari is nothing but a lump of muscle; It is just like the small tongue, a blot (disease) on the face.

82. O Brahmins! What is the use of those hands that do not clean the abode of the Lord? The hands of such an animal-like human are nothing but a burden on the shoulders.

Importance of Pradakshina & Namaskara:

83. Those legs which visit temples are indeed worthy. O auspicious one! That which see Lord Hari happily are the (only) real eyes.

84. O twice born! Even after being born (in this world), if one does not visit temples, what use are legs for such a person, who wanders around wastefully?.

85. O Dharmajna! Even for Rishis who are well versed in Veda and Vedangas, who are always reading/learning, who have their firm mind on Lord Hari, their Rishitva comes only due to the mercy of the Lord.

86. The pleasure of staying in sorrow-less Vaikunta, enjoying the comfort of cots laden with unique gems along with maidens, is the result of constant remembrance of Lord Keshava.

87. Even those who perform thousands of Ashwamedha sacrifices do not obtain the results that devotees of Lord Hari obtain!.

88. O People! Why all this effort in performing Yagnas and other rituals? Fold your hands towards the Lord. You will get Vaikunta, the abode of Lord Achyuta, merely by doing that!.

89. One who performs a Pradakshina, with devotion, even once to the plane of Lord Vishnu (his ratha and sanctum sanctorum) will obtain the results of performing thousands of Ashwamedha sacrifices.

90. One who performs Pradakshinas to Lord Hari with devotion will go to the abode of the Lord in a chariot driven by Hamsas.

91. The thousands of holy dips that people take at crores of holy waters (theertha kshetras) and the hundreds of observations of crores of rituals is not equal to even one sixteenth the result of devoutly offering salutations to Narayana.

92. Chest, head, eyes, mind, words (tongue), legs, hands and knees – since namaskara (prostration) is done with these eight parts, it is known as "ashtanga namaskara"

93. Even if one salutes Lord Hari, the wielder of Sharnga bow, out of pride and ego, the sins accumulated over hundreds of birth will be eliminated; this is certain!.

94. The One who is going to lift the people who are drowning in the ocean of life by continuously committing sins is none other than Lord Narayana, the Lord of the Universe and the Supreme One.

95. One will gain entry into Vishnu Loka and be worshiped there for as many years as the number of dust particles that stick to one's body while prostrating in front of Lord Vishnu!

Naivedya:

96. The naivedya (food) offered to Lord Vishnu is pure and fit for consumption. If one consumes the naivedya offered to other (lesser) Gods, one must undertake the Chaandraayana vrata (ritual).

97. The results one obtains by merely consuming the naivedya offered to Lord Vishnu is equal to the result obtained by performing thousands of crores of Chaandraayana vratas and crores of months of fasting.

98. One who consumes the naivedya after offering it to Lord Vishnu everyday will get the merits of hundreds of Chaandraayana vratas for every morsel of such food he consumes.

99. If, after offering it to Lord Murari, one consumes naivedya mixed with Tulasi and sprinkled with Vishnu Theertha, such a devotee will get the merits of having performed crores & crores of Yagnas.

100. If we accept the garland, gandha, clothes and jewellery adorned by you and we consume the food left over by you, then we, your eternal servants, will overcome Maya (Prakruti) [this is a quotation of Uddhava to Lord Krishna mentioned by Srimadacharya].

101. The flowers, food, fruits and water offered to Lord Rudra must not be touched (consumed). Shiva's nairmalya must not be crossed. Therefore, all the things offered to Rudra must be put into a well.

Tirtha of Vishnu:

102. One who takes bath in rivers which do not join seas gets the merits equivalent to performing yagas for three days; Bathing in rivers that do join seas gets merits equivalent to a fortnight; Bathing in the sea itself gets merits equivalent to a month.

103. River Godavari gives merits equal to Yagas performed for six months; River Ganga gives merits worth one year's performance of Yagas. But all these cannot give even one sixteenth the merits of the teertha of Lord Vishnu (Vishnu padodaka).

104. In order to get rid of sins, one needs to take the holy water from places such as Ganga, Gaya, Prayaga, Pushkara, Naimishaaranya and Kurukshetra for a long time; On the other hand, merely by taking the holy water of Lord Vishnu (tirtha), all the sins are instantly washed away!.

105. All the holy waters in this Universe are not equal to even one sixteenth the merit (power) of the water from Lord Vishnu's feet (Vishnu tirtha).

106. One who offers water to Lord Vishnu, consumes that water and also puts it on to his head will lose all his sins and obtain the siddhi (knowledge) of the Supreme Lord.

107. Brahma said:: One who offers Abhisheka (water) to a Shaligrama with the Dwadashakshara mantra "Om Namo Bhagavate Vasudevaya" and then takes (sprinkles on himself) that holy water will get the merit of having bathed in the holy River Ganga.

108. One who offers Abhisheka to Saligrama which has the Chakra signs on it (a – Sudarshana Saligrama, b – Saligrama and Dwaraka Chakrankita) and then sprinkles the water on to his head and drinks it will reach the abode of Vishnu.

109. The holy waters of Ganga, Godavari, Narmada and other rivers, which have the ability to destroy our Karmas and grant Moksha, always reside in the holy water of Shaligrama.

Shaligrama – Its Greatness:

110. The Shaligrama stone has signs of Chakra in it and has been made by a worm known as "Vajra Keeta". This stone has the special presence of Vishnu in it and rids one of all sins!.

111. Where Lord Keshava resides in the form of the Shaligrama Shila, in such a place all the devatas, suras, yajnas and the 14 worlds are present.

112. Even though there are all kinds of firewood in this world, when "Arani wood" is rubbed against each other, fire ignites. Similarly, even though Vishnu is present everywhere, His special presence radiates in Shaligrama.

113. The joy that Lord Hari derives out of staying in the chakras of Shaligrama stone – He does not derive the same joy even when He is with Lakshmi or when He is in Vaikunta.

114. O Vaishya! The stones that become available in the Shaligrama mountain are of twelve types. I will tell you the merits obtained by worshipping these stones according to the Shastras.

115. The merits that one gets by worshipping 12 crores Lingas for 12 Kalpas using Golden Lotuses is obtained by worshipping Shaligrama for just one day!

116. The Pitrus of one who performs Shraddha (ceremonies for the ancestors) near the Shaligrama stone (by having them) will enjoy the comforts of heaven for 100 Kalpas.

117. The Pitrus of one who performs Shraddha near the Shaligrama worshipped in ones home will be completely satisfied and obtain Moksha. This is certain!.

118. He alone qualifies as the true son who worships Lord Mahavishnu first and then worships/satisfies the devatas and Pitrus next with the remaining naivedya. "Let him live happily with his wife and children" will be the wish of devatas and Pitrus for such a person.

119. Padma purana:: Homas must be done and havis must be offered to other devatas only from the offerings made to Lord Vishnu. The same must be offered to Pitrus also. Unlimited merits are the result of doing so.

120. The Pitrus of a person who makes offerings first to his ancestors and then to the Paramatma will drink Retas and languish in hell in deep sorrow.

121.Garuda Purana:: If one gives the remaining Naivedya of Lord Hari to his Pitrus during Shraddha ceremony, the Pitrus of such a person will be satisfied for many crores of Kalpas with such a Pinda offering containing Tila and Kusha grass.

122.One who engages in fixing a price for Shaligrama stone; One who engages in selling Saligramas; One who allows trade involving Saligrama shilas; One who participates or approves the puchase of Shaligramas... (contd in next shloka)

123. (contd...) Such a person will attain hell after the Pralaya (armageddon) of this Universe. Therefore, wise men should give up (never engage) the trading of the Shaligrama Shila containing Chakras.

124. What more needs to be said? Those who are hesitant of sins have to worship Shaligrama. Those wishing for Moksha should always worship Shaligrama along with two Chakranikas (stones obtained in Dwaraka).

125. For a person who consumes the Tirtha made from Shaligrama Shila, what is the use of Panchagavya (mixture made using cow's milk, curds, ghee, gomutra and gomaya), even if consumed thousands of times!

126. Just as the tirtha of Vishnu is auspicious and gives merits, so does the nirmalya offered to Lord Hari (Tulasi, etc), His gandha, His naivedya, left-over dhoopa (angaara) and arathi also offer innumerable merits.

127. One should always consume the Naivedya which has the leaves of Tulasi (added to the food while offering it to the Lord). One should always bear, on his head, the Nirmalya as it remedies even the greatest sins!.

128. Irrespective of whether done with devotion or without devotion, if one sees or touches the Shaligrama stone which has Chakra signs on it, all the sins of an individual are washed away.

129. In the Shaligrama stone and the Chakranika stone from Dwaraka, the special presence of Lord Hari exists. Therefore, the tirtha made from these washes away even the sins of Brahma Hatya (killing of a knowledgeable man).

130. Where ever there is a Shaligrama stone, Lord Hari exists there. Hence, snana and daana made in such a place is a hundred times more beneficial than even Varanasi!.

131.O Bhudevi! Even if it is an impure place, or a country belonging to the Mlechhas, if there exists a Shaligrama which has Chakra signs on it, then a region of 3 yojanas around that place is my place (has my special presence).

132. Shaligrama contains the special presence of Lord Hari. Therefore, if one carries a Shaligrama with Chakra signs or a Chakranika to a place, that place becomes 100 times better than even Varanasi.

133. In Shaligrama stones and in Chakrankitas, there is always a special presence of the Lord. Hence, in any house where there is a confluence of these two, the Sadhaka there will surely obtain Mukti. This is certain!

Shankodaka & Nirmalya:

134. Rudra said:: The tirtha from the shankha, naivedya offered to Lord Hari, nirmalya, tirtha, arathi and angara (left-over from dhoopa) – these can relieve an individual from the sins of even brahma hatya.

135. If one rotates the shankha with water around Lord Hari from His feet to His head (known as shankha bhramana) and then sprinkles such water on to oneself, the sins corresponding to 10000 brahma hatyas will get burnt away.

136. If one has adorned himself with the shankha udaka (tirtha from shankha as explained in previous shloka), even navagrahas, bhootas, pisachas, snakes, rakshasas and other evil will run away from such a person.

137. The merits described in the shastras for performing monthly fasts for six months, the same merits can be obtained in kali yuga by consuming the food offered to Lord Vishnu.

138.If one cleans his body with the nirmalya offered to Lord Vishnu, the sins and diseases of such a person will completely get destroyed.

139. The sacred water from the feet of Vishnu (tirtha) will rid one from untimely deaths, deadly diseases and all sins and misfortune. The tirtha therefore is very auspicious.

Mangalarathi:

140. Rudra said:: O Devi! Listen to this amazing thing – The mangala arathi (auspicious lamp) held in front of Lord Vishnu, upon contact, burns away even the sins of brahma hatya (and other sins) of a person.

141. One who decorates himself with the angaraka (remains of dhoopa) offered to Lord Vishnu, the sins of such a person are washed away and diseases stay away from him.

Hari Sarvottamatva:

142. All the holy places on this earth that can give salvation can do so only because of the special presence of Lord Hari. That being the case, what is the use of such places to a realized person who sees the Supreme Being in everything?.

143. Even a person who shouts at a thief and repeatedly exclaims – "Hari (the one who takes away everything) is running!" will attain salvation just like a meritorious person. Note: "Hari" in Sanskrit also means "One who steals".

144. A person who neglects worship of Vishnu and worships other Gods is an ignorant who is discarding Amruta and accepting the deadly poison Halahala.

145. One who ignores Amruta and drinks ordinary water is a fool. Similarly, one who leaves Lord Hari and worships other Gods is also a fool.

146. That person who ignores Lord Hari and worships other Gods is like the person who leaves his own dharma (work – kaarya) and performs other dharma.

147. The sorry state of an ignorant who neglects Lord Hari and worships other Gods is like that of one who doesn't worship a cow but prays to a donkey!.

148. One who ignores Lord Hari and worships other Gods is like a thirsty fool who digs a well on the banks of the river Ganga.

149. Worshipping other Gods while leaving aside worship of Lord Hari is like drinking water from a well leaving the holy water of Ganga!.

150. Worshipping other Gods ignoring Lord Hari is like ignoring one's own mother while bowing to a characterless woman!.

Greatness of Human Life:

151. Till this physical body is in good condition, free from diseases and has active senses, perform that Sadhana which is good for you (i.e. worship of the Lord). Else, you will have to repent out of remorse later!.

152. Till the time your physical body has the strength and the senses are in condition, perform the worship of Govinda. Put your life to the best use by doing so.

153. When the senses (sense organs) are working well, put them into worshipping Hrishikesha, the Lord of the senses. Once the senses desert, who will (can) think of Hrishikesha?

154. Instead of thinking of material issues, which are like poison, if one devotes his time to the constant remembrance of Lord Vishnu, how will anyone not get out of the cycle of life?

155. The time one wastes in discussing & chatting worldly topics, if one spends the same time praying to Lord Vishnu, how would one not get out of the cycle of birth and death?.

Ekadashi:

156. Suta said:: Brahmins must learn about the day when Ekadashi occurs from astrologers who discuss and declare it. Having determined the same, fasting must be done on that day, else one will attain hell!.

157. If tithis are in Kshaya (less), excess or if all the three tithis occur on Ekadashi, then fasting done on Dwadashi is beneficial. The Ekadashi which has the contact of Dashami must be avoided.

158. If one fasts on an Ekadashi which has the contact of Dashami (i.e. Dashami exists at sunrise on the day), such a person will lose all the merits he has accumulated and will cause the destruction of his lineage and loss of all his wealth.

159. O excellent Brahmin! Just like Ganga water which has been contaminated by a drop of alcohol needs to be avoided, so should Ekadashi be avoided (for fasting) if there is even a faint contact with Dashami. (Note: Avoiding Ekadashi here means fasting on Dwadashi).

160. O excellent Brahmins! Just like Panchagavya, even though very pure, is avoided if it comes in contact with a dog's skin, so must Ekadashi be avoided if there is contact of Dashami, irrespective of whether it occurs in the Shukla

Paksha or Krishna Paksha.

161. O Brahmins! Therefore, one should never fast on an Ekadashi that comes with Dashami (Dashami at sunrise). Just as a fallen brahmin spoils the Shraddha ceremony, similarly all the accumulated merits get destroyed if one fasts on Viddhi Ekadashi.

162. Just like darkness vanishes upon sunrise, similarly if one observes Viddhi Ekadashi, all his merits accumulated due to previous Japa, Dana, Homa, Snana and worship of Lord Hari gets destroyed.

163. O Brahmin! If there is Dina Kshaya on the day of Ekadashi, then Dwadashi is the appropriate day for fasting and consequently Parana (breaking the fast) must be done on Trayodashi.

Notes: (a) If day starts with Navami, enters Dashami and later Ekadashi or (b) if Dashami exists for a while after sunrise or (c) if Ekadashi exists only for few ghatikas at sunrise and then Dwadashi starts – its termed Dina Kshaya. In such situations, fasting must be done on Dwadashi and Parana on subsequent day.

164. For padya (pratipad) and other days, it is considered auspicious and the counting starts from previous sunrise to next day's sunrise. But such a calculation is discarded for Harivasara (Ekadashi).

165. One should know that if one fasts on an Ekadashi when Dashami exists, even if only during Arunodaya (dawn), then such a fast will lead to accumulation of sins.

166. If Dashami tithi is observed during Arunodaya time and one still fasts on such an Ekadashi, it leads to destruction of Purusharthas such as Dharma, Artha and Kama. Therefore, there is no observance of Ekadashi on such a day.

167. The 4 ghatikas before sunrise (4 x 24 minutes) is known as "Arunodaya Kala". For yatis, this is the most appropriate time for bathing. The shastras proclaim this time to be as pure as the Ganga.

168. O Brahmins! If Ekadashi exists for 2 muhurthas (4 ghatikas) before sunrise, then such an Ekadashi is called Sampurna Ekadashi and fasting must be observed on the same day.

169. If Ekadashi exists only for 3 ghatikas before sunrise, then such an Ekadashi is called Sandighdha Ekadashi. Fasting must be avoided on this day as it can cause destruction of Dharma and Artha.

170. When there is Viddhi Ekadashi, fasting must be done on Dwadashi for the betterment of one's children and grandchildren. Similarly, Parana must be done on Trayodashi. This will give the merits of hundreds of Yagas.

171. If Ekadashi exists for just 2 ghatikas before sunrise, it is considered as Sankeerna Ekadashi. Those desirous of Dharma and Artha should not fast on such Ekadashis.

172. Having fasted on an Ekadashi which had Dashami at the beginning, Gandhari lost all her 100 sons. Therefore, Viddhi Ekadashi must be avoided.

173. The learned say that Ekadashi with even a small element of Dashami must be avoided just like Amruta which is contaminated with alcohol is avoided.

174. Many shastras offer contrasting rules about Ekadashi. If brahmins are discussing about when to fast, it is always better (safer) to fast on Dwadashi and perform Parana on Trayodashi.

175. If Ekadashi has the Vedha of Dashami, even if the nakshatra during Dwadashi is Shravana, it is correct to fast on Dwadashi, both during Shukla and Krishna pakshas.

176. Thousands of eclipses, ten thousand Vyatipatas, lakhs of Amavasyas; all these are not equal to even one sixteenth of a Dwadashi.

177. Even if there is a bit of Dwadashi on a Trayodashi, it is just as fit for fasting like a pure Dwadashi (full day of Dwadashi). Dashami is like poison while Ekadashi is like Amruta. Therefore, Ekadashi which is contact with poison-like Dashami must be avoided and Ekadashi, which is nectar-like, must always be accepted for fasting.

178. Those who fast on a Viddhi Ekadashi and perform Parana on the next day (Dwadashi) are fools and attain hell!.

179. Those shastras which propagate fasting on a Viddhi Ekadashi are oriented towards material gains such as wealth. Ekadashi which has the vedha of Dashami is never pleasing to Lord Hari.

180. On the other hand, upon the prayer of Mohini, wife of King Rukmangada, Lord Janardana, in the form of Veda Vyasa wrote those statements in the Puranas which propagate fasting on a Viddhi Ekadashi, just in order to confuse the evil!.

181.The worship of lesser Gods who will grant (only) material wealth should increase. The wealth of evil people should get destroyed. The ignorance and incorrect knowledge of Asuras should increase. Pashandas should increase. These people should not get the true knowledge of the Supreme Being. Moksha should be unattainable by them. (Hence HE wrote some wrong statements in the Puranas). •

182. In this way, if one discards Viddhi Ekadashi and observes fast on Dwadashi, by that single observance, the sins accumulated over crores of births will get destroyed.

183.If one observes Ekadashi in spite of resistance or obstruction from others, such a person will get a crore times more merits than one who merely fasts. Not only the sins accumulated over eternity...(contd in next shloka).

184........but also the sins that one can potentially accumulate over subsequent births also get destroyed, if one gets another person to start observing Ekadashi fasting. There is no other person who is more liked by Lord Hari or me (Rudra).

185. If there is no Vedha for Ekadashi, the Parana on Dwadashi must never be compromised. For Parana and Marana, the particular Tithi at that time must be considered, so say the Shastras.

(Note – (1) This shloka means that if no Vedha, fasting must necessarily be done on Ekadashi and consequently Parana on Dwadashi. (2) Here Marana refers to the time to be considered for performing Shraddha for departed ancestors).

186. Bachelors, householders, people retired from active life and sanyasis, brahmins, kshatriyas, vaishyas and shudras, sumangalis...(contd in next shloka)

187. .... widows, those outside of the 4 varnas such as sutas, vaidehikas and others also should, without fail, observe Ekadashi during both shukla and krishna pakshas.

188. Due to ignorance or wrong knowledge, if one consumes food on either a Shukla Ekadashi or Krishna Ekadashi, such a person will definitely obtain hell.

189. Those people who think of only Shukla Paksha Ekadashi as fit for fasting and, out of ignorance, think that Krishna Paksha Ekadashi does not warrant fasting are sinners who will go to hell. This is certain!.

190. Shankara said:: O dear one! Whether it is black or white, a cow must never be killed. Similarly, whether it is Shukla Paksha or Krishna Paksha, one must never eat on an Ekadashi.

191. Statements such as Ekadashi not to be performed in Krishna Paksha, fasting not to be done on Ekadashi with Bharani Nakshatra and other such forbidden rules exist only for those who observe Ekadashi with the goal of materialistic results.

192. Those who fast for materialistic desires also should fast on every Ekadashi (without exceptions) for obtaining Moksha and their wishes. This is for pleasing the Supreme Lord and not with the intention of any particular desire.

193. Therefore, whether it is Shukla Paksha or Krishna Paksha, or even if there is Bharani Nakshatra or any other reason, one must always fast on an Ekadashi in order to obtain the love of Lord Hari and also attain his abode.

194. On the day after Dwadashi (Trayodashi), if there is Dwadashi for a ghatika or even a Kala (24 seconds), doing Parana (breaking fast) on previous day (Dwadashi) will destroy the merits accumulated due to 12 Dwadashi Paranas.

Note: If there is any contact of Dwadashi with Trayodashi next day, fasting must be done on 2 days and Parana must be done on Trayodashi.

195.If one does not fast on an Atirikta Dwadashi (excess Dwadashi on Trayodashi) or if Dwadashi is over at the time of Parana on Trayodashi, one loses the merits accumulated over 12 Dwadashi Paranas.

196. If there is excess Dwadashi on the day of Trayodashi and one still eats on the previous Dwadashi day or if one does not perform Parana on the morning of such a Trayodashi when Dwadashi still exists, the merits accumulated over

12 Dwadashi Paranas will be destroyed.

197. If one does not fast on a Dwadashi which comes along with Shravana Nakshatra, such an dumb person will lose all merits accumulated over 5 years.

Note: Shravana Nakshatra and Dwadashi tithi should coincide till only noon. If Shravana Nakshatra extends to Trayodashi, fasting must not be done on such a Dwadashi.

198. If one fasts on Ekadashi and also fasts on the Dwadashi (in case of Shravana Dwadashi), then missing Dwadashi Parana will not count as a mistake. After all, isn't Lord Hari the Lord of both the days?

199. How can one perform proper parana if dwadashi exists for only a very short time? (Answer) There is no mistake if one does Parana initially with just water and then has a proper meal.

200. If there is very little Dwadashi left, one should perform all his morning rituals AND rituals of the noon before dawn itself. The meal which is consumed later will attract distortion (in terms of merits).

201. If one is unable to practise Dwadashi Parana as previously described, one should perform Parana with water first and then consume food. So say some.

202. If one drinks water, it is equivalent to both eating as well as staying without food, so say the knowledgeable. Hence, I will perform the vrata of Dwadashi Parana with just water (one must perform Sankalpa in this way).

203. Neither Kashi, nor Gaya; neither Ganga nor Narmada; neither Godavari nor Kurukshetra. None of them are equal to the day of Lord Hari.

204. Neither thousands of Ashwamedha sacrifices nor hundreds of Vajapeya sacrifices are equivalent to even one sixteenth the merits of fasting on an Ekadashi.

205. O Excellent King! The firewood, which are our sins, accumulated over hundreds of births are instantly burnt to ashes by the fire, which is the merit obtained, due to fasting on an Ekadashi!.

206. There is no other day on this earth which is as purifying and capable of destroying our sins as the day of Lord Padmanabha.

207. O King! Sins accumulate and stay in this human body only until one fasts on the day of Lord Padmanabha.

208. O Lord! All the sins committed by the eleven sense organs are destroyed by fasting on the eleventh day (Ekadashi).

Note: The 11 sense organs are eyes, ears, nose, tongue, skin, mouth, hands, legs, renal and excretory organs and the mind.

209. O King! There is nothing else that is equivalent to Ekadashi in destroying one's sins. Even if one observes Ekadashi just for showing off, such a person shall not see Yama.

210. Lord Veda Vyasa said:: On my day (Ekadashi), even if one offers me a little food, such a person will attain hell. What then of a person who actually consumes food himself!.

211. Lord Veda Vyasa said:: One who consumes food on Ekadashi, be it in Shukla Paksha or Krishna Paksha, will get the sins of Brahma Hatya, Go Hatya, thieving, Gurupatni Gamana, and others.

212. Sleeping with one's own mother, consuming beef, killing a Brahmin, drinking alchohol – even these are ok when compared with consuming food on Ekadashi.

Note: This comparison is only used for highlighting the importance of Ekadashi fasting and is not a judgement on those immoral activities in any way.

213. People who consume food on the auspicious day of Ekadashi are the lowest amongst humans. If one sees the inauspicious face of such people, one should watch the Sun (to cleanse oneself).

214. All the big sins on this earth, such as Brahma Hatya and others, take shelter and reside in food on the day of Lord Hari.

215. Rukmangada said:: A person who is above eight years of age and less than eighty and consumes food on the day of Lord Vishnu, such a person is a big sinner!.

216. Be it one's father, son, wife or friend, one who consumes food on the day of Lord Padmanabha is a criminal and qualifies for punishment.

217. Dharma Vibhushana said:: O devotees! Tomorrow morning is Ekadashi. Hence, today, do not consume any kshara substances (cotyledons). Do not consume even salt. Stick to only havish foods (milk, curds, fruits, amla, etc).

218. Do not have physical intercourse with your wife today. Sleep on the floor and constantly think of him who is the Lord of Brahma and others, the one who has been ever-present, the one who is the best amongst Purushas!.

219. On Dashami, have food only once. On Ekadashi, observe complete fasting and do not perform rituals such as Shraddha, Tilodaka, Pinda Pradhana and Jala Tharpana.

220. Brahma and Vyasa said:: On the holy day of Dwadashi, the day that destroys all sins, the ones who perform Upavasa shall never see Yama or Naraka. Such people will never undergo suffering in hell!

Upasamhara and Mangala:

Three amazing avatars of Lord Vayudeva are Hanuma,Bhima and Madhwa. The first avatar of hanuman carried the words of Lord Rama to Seeta. The second avatar of bhima destroyed the army of the kauravas. The third avatar of madhwa has composed this creation to obtain the grace of Lord Keshava.

Let this work, which is like the rays of the glowing sun called anandatirtha, and which is like bright rays absorbed by even the devatas, grant all the good desires of ours.